# Hey Kids! Let's Visit Washington DC

**Teresa Mills**

Life Experiences Publishing

Bluff City, Tennessee

## Companion Activity Book Series

Make your trip to Washington DC even more fun and educational with our companion activity books. The series includes:

- An Activity / Game Book
- A Coloring Book
- A Travel Journal

Check these out here:

https://kid-friendly-family-vacations.com/wdcpkg

Teresa Mills/Life Experiences Publishing
PO Box 53
Bluff City, TN 37618
kid-friendly-family-vacations.com

Book Layout © 2014 BookDesignTemplates.com

Hey Kids! Let's Visit Washington DC/ Teresa Mills.-- 1st ed.
ISBN-13: 978-1-946049-07-0

# Contents

Welcome.....................................................1

A Little about Washington DC .......................3

The White House (Where the President Lives).5

The United States Capitol (Where Congress Meets) ........................................................9

The National Cathedral (The National House of Prayer) .....................................................13

The Arlington National Cemetery.................17

The National Mall and Reflecting Pool..........23

Washington DC Monuments: The Washington Monument...............................................27

Washington DC Monuments: The Lincoln Memorial..................................................31

Washington DC Monuments: The Jefferson Memorial..................................................35

The National Air and Space Museum............39

The National Museum of Natural History ......43

The National Museum of American History....47

The Bureau of Engraving and Printing (US Money Printed Here).................................49

Ford's Theater .........................................53

The National Zoo (Washington Zoo) ...........57

Getting Around Washington DC – The
Washington DC Metro ...................................61

Thank You ..............................................63

Acknowledgements .....................................65

# Preface

## Welcome

My family and I have traveled for many years, and Washington DC is one of our favorite places to visit. There are just so many things to do and see there. We have visited many times, but never seem to really see everything!

The book is written as a fun fact guide about the Washington DC monuments, museums, and statues. The book includes some Washington DC history interspersed with fun facts about the things to do in Washington DC. The book can easily be shared with younger children as well through reading with them.

You can visit Washington DC right from your own home with this book! You can enjoy this book whether you are preparing for a Washington DC vacation with the family and want to learn more about the town, or just enjoy the book and pictures to learn a little more about Washington DC attractions.

I hope you enjoy this book, and use it to learn a little more about the capitol of the United States of America.

When you take your family trip to Washington DC, I have a free gift for you!

http://kid-friendly-family-vacations.com/wdcattractions

When you have finished this book, I invite you to look at the other books in the series:

*Hey Kids! Let's Visit A Cruise Ship*
*Hey Kids! Let's Visit New York City*
*Hey Kids! Let's Visit London England*
*Hey Kids! Let's Visit San Francisco*
*Hey Kids! Let's Visit Savannah Georgia*
*Hey Kids! Let's Visit Paris France*
*Hey Kids! Let's Visit Charleston South Carolina*

Enjoy!

Teresa Mills

# Introduction

# A Little about Washington DC

Washington DC is the Capitol of the United States of America. DC stands for "District of Columbia".

Washington DC is not a part of any U.S. state. It is a federal district under the exclusive jurisdiction of the U.S. congress.

Washington DC was formed with land donated by both Maryland and Virginia and was named in honor of George Washington.

Washington DC is home to the President of the United States of America as well as Congress – the governing body of the USA.

In addition to the government buildings around town, there are many museums, memorials, and monuments throughout – there is even a two mile long park right in the center of downtown.

So kids...Let's Visit Washington DC!!!

# 1

# The White House (Where the President Lives)

The White House is the home and workplace of the President of the United States of America. It is located at 1600 Pennsylvania Avenue in Washington DC.

The White House Complex includes the Residence (where the President and his family lives), the West Wing and the East Wing. The part of the White House that the President and his family live in is called the Executive Residence. On either side of the Residence is a building called a wing. There is the West Wing and the East Wing.

The West Wing Is where the President's offices are located. The President's staff and several other employees have offices in the West Wing as well.

The President's cabinet meets in the West Wing, and the Situation Room is located there as well. The Situation Room is where the President, the cabinet, and military advisors meet and plan during a time of crisis.

The East Wing has other offices in it. The East Wing sometimes houses the office of The First Lady, and is also where the White House social office is located.

This is the front of the White House. In the picture you see the Executive Residence. If you were walking on Pennsylvania Avenue in Washington DC, this the view you would have of the White House.

*The front of the White House*

The back of the White House is shown below. When the President takes the helicopter (Marine One) to and from the White House, it lands in the back yard of the House.

Would it be cool or not cool to be able to get to your house in a helicopter?

*The back of the White House*

What would you think if you walked around the corner, and saw this house?

## Fun Facts About The White House

- Every President since 1800 has lived in The White House.
- There is a bunker under the East Wing that was built during World War II
- The White House appears on the back of the twenty dollar bill.

# 2

## The United States Capitol (Where Congress Meets)

The United States Capitol Building is where the United States Congress meets. The Congress is made up of the Senate and the House of Representatives.

The Capitol Building looks a lot like the White House because it was designed at the same time. There was a competition in 1792 to design the President's home and the building that the congress would meet in. The prize for the design competition was $500 and a piece of land in the DC area.

Do you think $500 was a lot of money in 1792? That would be over $12,000 in our time.

Construction began on September 18, 1793 with George Washington laying the cornerstone. The Senate wing was completed in 1800 and the House of Representatives wing was completed in 1811. The House of Representatives met in a temporary wooden pavilion in the meantime.

There is also a reflecting pool in front of the Capitol. In the right light, the US capitol is reflected very nicely on the water.

What do you think about the reflection below?

*The Capitol reflected in the Reflecting Pool*

*The US Capitol*

## Fun Facts About The United States Capitol

- Thomas Jefferson decided to call this building The Capitol rather than "Congress House".
- In 1850, after the Senate and House wings were added, the dome had to be rebuilt since it was too small for the new building.
- Presidential Inaugurations are held at the US Capitol every four years.

# 3

---

# The National Cathedral (The National House of Prayer)

The Washington National Cathedral is a part of the Episcopal Church. The United States Congress has named the Cathedral the "National House of Prayer".

Worship services are held at the National Cathedral every day of the year. There are four or five services per day, depending on the season.

As the National House of Prayer, the Cathedral has been used for memorial services such as a memorial for the Vietnam Veterans and a memorial for the victims of the September 11, 2001 terror attacks.

The National Cathedral has been used for the funerals of several American Presidents such as Dwight Eisenhower, Ronald Reagan, and Gerald Ford.

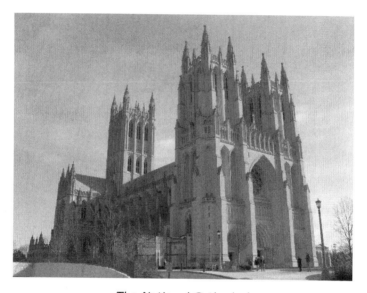

*The National Cathedral*

## Fun Facts About The National Cathedral

- There are 200 stained glass windows in the Cathedral.
- These stained glass windows commemorate events in American History.
    - The Lewis and Clark Expedition
    - US astronauts landing on the moon
- The Cathedral has two full sets of bells and the bells are rung by "The Washington Ringing Society"

# 4

# The Arlington National Cemetery

The Arlington National Cemetery is a "United States Military Cemetery". It is a 624 acre cemetery located just across the Potomac River from Washington DC in Arlington, Virginia.

The cemetery was started during the Civil War, and is the final resting place for America's military, beginning with Civil War soldiers.

The cemetery is laid out beautifully, with all head stones in neat lines.

*The Arlington National Cemetery*

The Arlington National Cemetery is the home of the Tomb of the Unknowns. This is a memorial to all American soldiers who died in war, but were unidentified. Written on the side of the Tomb is:

**"Here rests in honored glory an American soldier known but to God"**

The Tomb of the Unknowns has been guarded continually (day and night) since July 2, 1937. Guarding the Tomb of the Unknowns is an honor, and taken very seriously by the young soldiers who have the job!

The guarding of the Tomb of the Unknowns is a very precise military operation. If you are interested in learning more about the men and women who guard the tomb, take a look at this website – it explains about "Walking the Mat" and how the guards prepare for the job.

https://kid-friendly-family-vacations.com/tomb

What do you think? Would you like to be one of the soldiers who guards the Tomb of the Unknowns?

*The Tomb of the Unknowns*

## Fun Facts About Arlington National Cemetery

- The most visited memorial at the cemetery is the grave site of President John F Kennedy. There is an Eternal Flame at his grave site.
- There are close to 30 funerals at Arlington Cemetery every day.
- Some other Memorials at the Cemetery:
    - Memorial for the Space Shuttle Challenger
    - Memorial for Pan Am Flight 103

# 5

# The National Mall and Reflecting Pool

The National Mall is a really cool National Park in downtown Washington DC. The park runs for 1.9 miles, from the steps of the Capitol Building to the Lincoln Memorial. There are about 24 million visitors to the National Mall each year.

The reflecting pool is actually called the Lincoln Memorial Reflecting Pool and spans most of the distance between the Lincoln Memorial to the Washington Monument. Depending on where you stand, you might be able to see either the Lincoln Memorial or the Washington Monument reflected in the pool. The reflecting pool is lined by walking paths and shade trees on both sides.

Can you see the Washington Monument reflected in the picture?

*The National Mall Reflecting Pool*

The National Mall was set up so that there would always be an area for recreation and enjoyment of people in downtown Washington DC, and to provide a monumental, dignified, and symbolic setting for the museums, memorials, and government buildings along the mall.

At any point in time that you may be visiting the National Mall, there are people having lunch, running, playing football and simply enjoying the area. The Smithsonian Carousel, located on the Mall, is always popular with the kids!

The National Mall is used for many other things than just the park. The Mall is used for civic gatherings, gathering for presidential inaugurations (for people without official tickets), celebrations, concerts, and just about anything you can imagine!

The National Mall is lined with museums and memorials as well. Here is some of what you will find along the mall...

- National Museum of American History
- National Museum of Natural History
- National Gallery of Art Sculpture Garden
- National Gallery of Art
- National Museum of the American Indian
- National Air and Space Museum
- Smithsonian Institution Building ("The Castle")
- Freer Gallery of Art
- United States Capitol and its ground
- Ulysses S. Grant Memorial
- Capitol Reflecting Pool
- Washington Monument and its grounds
- Lincoln Memorial
- Lincoln Memorial Reflecting Pool
- World War II Memorial
- Korean War Veterans Memorial
- Vietnam Veterans Memorial
- The Three Soldiers Statue
- Vietnam Women's Memorial

# 6

## Washington DC Monuments: The Washington Monument

The Washington Monument stands on the National Mall in Washington DC and is a memorial for the first president of the United States, George Washington.

The structure is an obelisk, which is a tall, four-sided, narrow tapering monument that ends in a pyramid-like shape at the top. Have you EVER heard of an obelisk? I never have!

The monument was built in two phases. The first phase was from 1848 to 1858. It was only built to 152 feet during this phase. The second phase was from 1878 to 1888. That's a gap of twenty years in which the monument sat unfinished.

Did you hear that kids? Twenty years?!?!? Can you imagine a partially completed monument standing in the middle of a city?

The Washington Monument opened to the public on October 9, 1888.

Visitors can go inside the monument with a ticket. (Tickets are free and are given out the same day). Visitors ride an elevator to the top where there are small windows to view the surrounding area.

On the picture, can you see the two different colors of the monument? This shows the twenty year span in time between constructions.

## Fun Facts About The Washington Monument

- It is the world's largest obelisk.
- It is 555 feet 5 1/8 inches tall.
- The elevator ride to the top of the monument takes only 70 seconds.
- The elevator ride back to the bottom takes 2 minutes because it stops along the way to show riders some of the interior of the monument.

*The Washington Monument*

# 7

# Washington DC Monuments: The Lincoln Memorial

The Lincoln Memorial is a memorial to Abraham Lincoln, the 16th President of the United States of America. It is located on the western end of the National Mall, across the reflecting pool from the Washington Monument.

The monument building is large and inside it is a large seated sculpture of Abraham Lincoln. Also in the building are inscriptions of two of the most well-known speeches by Lincoln...The Gettysburg Address and his Second Inaugural Address.

The Lincoln Memorial was dedicated in 1922.

*The Lincoln Memorial*

The architect of the memorial was Henry Bacon and the painter of the interior murals was Jules Guerin.

The sculptor of the primary statue – Abraham Lincoln, 1920 – was Daniel Chester French.

## Fun Facts About The Lincoln Memorial

- Approximately 6 million people visit the memorial annually.
- The memorial is depicted on the back of the five dollar bill and the penny.
- Martin Luther King delivered his "I Have a Dream" speech at the memorial on August 28, 1963.

*The Lincoln Memorial Sculpture*

# 8

# Washington DC Monuments: The Jefferson Memorial

The Jefferson Memorial is dedicated to Thomas Jefferson, the main drafter and writer of the "Declaration of Independence". Thomas Jefferson was the third President of the United States of America.

The monument is in West Potomac Park, across the Tidal Basin from the Lincoln Memorial. Around the memorial are many Japanese cherry trees. These trees were a gift from people of Japan in 1912.

*The Jefferson Memorial*

The Jefferson Memorial was built starting in 1939 and was completed in 1943. The bronze statue of Thomas Jefferson was added in 1947.

It's a pretty impressive looking memorial, isn't it?

## Fun Facts About The Jefferson Memorial

- Lines from the Declaration of Independence can be found on the southwest panel.
- This memorial does not get as many visitors annually as those on the National Mall.
- The steps leading up to the memorial are made of pure marble.

*The Jefferson Memorial*

# 9

# The National Air and Space Museum

The main campus of the National Air and Space Museum is on the National Mall and is one of the museums of the Smithsonian Institution. It opened its main building to the public in 1976 and gets close to 7 million visitors a year!

The museum holds the largest collection of historic aircraft and spacecraft in the world!

Not only is this a museum, it is a center for research into the history and science of aviation and spaceflight, as well as planetary science and terrestrial geology and geophysics. Big words, I know!

When my family visited the museum, we were able to participate in a paper airplane contest. It was really cool. We made our own paper airplane, and then took turns tying to fly it through a tire across the room. I didn't do very well, but it was pretty cool to see what everyone came up with!

Inside the museum, there are exhibits all about American space and air flight, including astronauts' suits and aircraft.

## Fun Facts About The National Air and Space Museum

- More than 8 million people visit the museum per year.
- The museum has over 60,000 items in its collection
- The collection includes Saturn V rockets. Jetliners, gliders, and space helmets.
- One third of the museum's collection are one of a kind or related to a major milestone.

# 10

## The National Museum of Natural History

The National Museum of Natural History is part of the Smithsonian Institution and is located on the National Mall in Washington DC. This museum is dedicated to the knowledge of the natural world!

The museum has over 570,000 catalogued reptiles from around the world. The gem collection includes some of the most famous pieces of gems and minerals in the world, including the Hope Diamond.

*The National Museum of Natural History*

There are many different animal displays in the museum as well!

The Dinosaur Exhibit in the Natural History Museum has fossilized skeletons and cast models, including a Tyrannosaurus rex cast facing a Triceratops cast.

*The skeleton of a T-Rex*

**Fun Facts About The National Museum of Natural History**

- At 8 million visitors per year, it is the most visited of all Smithsonian museums
- The museum is home to about 185 professional natural history scientists — the largest group of scientists dedicated to the study of natural and cultural history in the world.

# 11

# The National Museum of American History

The National Museum of American History is also located on the National Mall in Washington DC. Its main purpose is to preserve and display the heritage of the United States in the areas of social, political, cultural, scientific and military history.

This museum features a bit of just about everything you can imagine from American History... from television shows we watch to recreation and vacation trends... even school lunch boxes.

There are many displays telling the history of American history such as the history of transportation in the USA.

## Fun Facts About The National American History Museum

- The museum displays Taking America to Lunch, which celebrates the history of American lunch boxes.
- The museum displays the original Star Spangled Banner, which was inspired by Francis Scott Key's poem.

# 12

## The Bureau of Engraving and Printing (US Money Printed Here)

The Bureau of Engraving and Printing is where the currency of the United States is printed…. Literally!

In addition to printing money, the bureau also prints award certificates; invitations and admission cards; and many different types of identification cards, forms, and other special security - really, just about anything that the U.S. government needs.

The process of printing and keeping track of the US currency is a big project.

- Currency paper is 25% linen and 75% cotton. It has red and blue synthetic fibers of various lengths distributed evenly throughout the paper. Before World War I the fibers were made of silk.
- Currency is printed with a process called Intaglio Printing which causes the surface of the note to feel slightly raised, and the reverse side to feel slightly indented.
- The notes (paper money currency) are inspected for any defects after the printing process. The notes are then overprinted to add the Federal Reserve District seal and its corresponding number designation with black ink, and the Treasury seal and serial numbers in green ink.
- If a defect is found after the serial number printing process, that bill is replaced with a "star note". The "star note" looks just like

the original bills, but the serial numbers are different, and there is a star after the serial number. The defective serial number is not used again.

Pretty cool, isn't it?

## Fun Facts About The Bureau of Engraving and Printing

- In the gift shop, you can purchase full sheets of un-cut currency.
- You can tour the bureau daily Monday – Friday.

# 13

# Ford's Theater

Ford's Theater is a historic, operating theater in Washington DC. There have been plays in the theater since the 1860's.

It is also the site of the assassination of President Abraham Lincoln on April 14, 1865.

After being shot, the fatally wounded president was carried across the street to the Petersen House, where he died the next morning.

The National Park Service has operated the Petersen House as a historic house museum since 1933. The rooms have been furnished to appear as if it were the night of Abraham Lincoln's death.

The Petersen House and Ford's Theater are a National Historic Site and are open for tours. The box

*Ford's Theater*

seat where President Lincoln was seated during the play is preserved.

## Fun Facts About Ford's Theater

- The building that houses the theater was originally a house of worship for the First Baptist Church of Washington.
- Lincoln and his wife were seeing the play Our American Cousin the night he was shot.
- The theater has been renovated several times.  The last time was in the 2000's.  It re-opened on February 11, 2009, which is also when we commemorated Lincoln's 200th birthday.

# 14

## The National Zoo (Washington Zoo)

Formally named The National Zoological Park, The National Zoo in Washington DC is a part of the Smithsonian Institute. This zoo is one of the oldest zoos in the United States!

The Zoo in Washington is one of the best around and one of only four zoos in the US that have pandas. The panda exhibit at the zoo is called the "Great Panda Habitat"!

*The Great Panda at The National Zoo*

The gorillas in the "Great Ape House" are very personable as well. The gorillas, like the one in the picture, like to watch the visitors to the zoo and sometimes make fun of them. It is pretty fun to watch.

*Gorilla at the National Zoo*

There are orangutans as well in the Great Ape House. The orangutans are allowed cross over to the "Think Tank" freely. They travel back and forth on cables above the ground.

What's the Think Tank at a zoo, you ask?

The Think Tank is an area designed to educate visitors about how animals think and learn about their surroundings. It has several interactive displays that teach visitors how zoologists conduct their studies.

## Fun Facts About The National Zoo

- The National Zoo is home to over 2,000 different animals that represent more than 400 species. Almost a quarter of all animals in this zoo are on the endangered species list.
- There is a mobile app from the zoo that you can download – it shows feeding times and has some information about the animals.
- The main campus of the zoo is 163 acres and it's a twenty minute metro ride from the National Mall.

# 15

# Getting Around Washington DC – The Washington DC Metro

The metro is the rapid transport system in Washington DC. The Metro network consists of six lines, 91 stations, and 118 miles (190 km) of route throughout the city and surrounding areas.

The metro is an easy and quick way to get around the city and surrounding area!

Have you ever ridden a train on a mass transit system in a city?   In major cities, this might be the way you would get to school.

Here is a metro train at a station. There are usually more people around.

*Washington DC Metro Trains at the Station*

## Fun Facts About The Washington DC Metro

- The word "metro" actually comes from an abbreviated form of the "Paris Metropolitan".
- It is illegal to eat, drink, or smoke on the Washington D.C. metro because of the extra costs associated with cleaning the carpet. Yup, THE CARPET.
- Metro is the second-busiest rapid transit system in the United States in number of passenger trips, after the New York City Subway.

# Thank You

Thank you for purchasing and taking the time to read this book.

This is the first in the "Hey Kids! Let's Visit" series of book for children.

To keep in touch and be notified of the next books in the series, please join us:

http://kid-friendly-family-vacations.com/wdcattractions

---

**Companion Activity Book Series**

Make your trip to Washington DC even more fun and educational with our companion activity books. The series includes:

- An Activity / Game Book
- A Coloring Book
- A Travel Journal

Check these out here:
https://kid-friendly-family-vacations.com/wdcpkg

Thanks again!

If you enjoyed this book, I invite you to check out the other books in the Hey Kids! Let's Visit Series

*Hey Kids! Let's Visit A Cruise Ship*
*Hey Kids! Let's Visit New York City*
*Hey Kids! Let's Visit London England*
*Hey Kids! Let's Visit San Francisco*
*Hey Kids! Let's Visit Savannah Georgia*
*Hey Kids! Let's Visit Paris France*
*Hey Kids! Let's Visit Charleston South Carolina*

Teresa Mills

# Acknowledgements

**Proof-reading / Editing** - Marcia Reagan

**Cover Photos**

White House Photo -  © tiger_barb / deposit photos

Airplane Photo - © Andrew Mills

Elephant in Museum Photo - © Andrew Mills

**Photos in Book**

Front of White House - © tiger_barb / deposit photos

Back of White House – © Vacclav / deposit photos

US Capitol – © Camrocker / Deposit Photos

US Capitol reflecting - © sborisov/123rf.com

National Cathedral – © Tammy Brewer

Arlington Cemetery – © SOMATUSCANI / Deposit Photos

Arlington Cemetery – Tomb of Unknowns – © izanbar / Deposit Photos

National Mall (Reflection) – © lunamarina / Deposit Photos

Washington Monument - © Curioso_Travel_Photography / Deposit Photos

Lincoln Memorial – © kmiragaya / Deposit Photos

Lincoln Memorial -statue - © Funniefarm5 / Deposit Photos

Jefferson Memorial – © kimshanephoto / deposit Photos

Jefferson Memorial - statue – © slickspics / Deposit Photos

National Air and Space Museum (2 photos) - © Andrew Mills

National Museum of Natural History (Elephant) - © Andrew Mills

National Museum of Natural History (T-Rex) - © Chitsanupong Chuenthananont/123rf.com

Bureau of Engraving and Printing - © 4kclips / Deposit Photos

Ford's Theater - © dpfoxfoto / Deposit Photos

National Zoo Panda - ©Natalia Bratslavsky /123rf.com

National Zoo Gorilla - ©Hal Brindley/123rf.com

Washington DC Metro - © czuber / Deposit Photos

# ABOUT THE AUTHOR

Teresa Mills is the best selling author of the "Hey Kids! Let's Visit..." Book Series for Kids!

Teresa's goal through her books and website is to help parents / grand-parents who want to build the life experiences of their children / grand-children through travel and learning activities.

She is an active mother and Mimi. She and her family love traveling in the USA, and internationally too! They love exploring new places, eating cool foods, and having yet another adventure as a family! With the Mills, it's all about traveling as family.

In addition to traveling, Teresa enjoys reading, hiking, biking, and helping others.

Join in the fun at kid-friendly-family-vacations.com

Made in the USA
Middletown, DE
01 June 2019